Initiation to economic modeling

Diana Loubaki

Initiation to economic modeling

To Charles Casier Senior

Presentation

This book applies Romer (1990)' work untitled "endogenous technological change" to a country endowed with a low or a zero technological level in order to describe the process of economic development.

The main purpose of the book is to show how to get used to economic modeling. Therefore, the proof is conducted step by step in order to highlight theoretical foundations methodology leading to understand a given economic phenomenon.

In spite of the subject, the main focus of the book is to initiate to fundamental economic analysis. The purpose of the

To Charles Casier Senior

Presentation

This book applies Romer (1990)' work untitled "endogenous technological change" to a country endowed with a low or a zero technological level in order to describe the process of economic development.

The main purpose of the book is to show how to get used to economic modeling. Therefore, the proof is conducted step by step in order to highlight theoretical foundations methodology leading to understand a given economic phenomenon.

In spite of the subject, the main focus of the book is to initiate to fundamental economic analysis. The purpose of the book is to be able to use theoretical methodology in order to get answers to several economic questions. The key of the methodology remains on the assumptions made to build models.

The subject and the style used in this book are conventional. But the originality of the book comes from its goal which is to initiate to fundamental economic research tools.

Introduction

The analysis develops a dynamic growth process of a little country which desires economic development through knowledge increase. The economic development strategy based on knowledge increase requires international exchange based on innovations and training in new technologies.

We evidence the required steps of fundamental economic modeling methodology. Crucially based on assumptions on economic agents' behaviors as well as on economic environment over time, the whole constitutes macroeconomic principles of global economic system. Finally results are obtained though the *Walrasian* general equilibrium equation where if $n-1$ markets are in equilibrium, then the nth market is also in equilibrium. Indeed the history is summarized by a single equation which predicts the long run outcomes of the economic system though crucial variables. The interest of doing so is to understand the central problem through the history in order to anticipate its future.

FIRST PART

Endogenous technological change

Chapitre N° 1

The Preliminary Analysis

1   PRESENTATION

The analysis is conducted on the basis of Romer (1990) results, a growth model where technology is endogenous i.e technological change results from the decisions of the agents who maximize their profits. The adaptation of this model to our study means that, technology character of inputs of production can be partially or completely "endogenous". The entrepreneur's behavior and market size are the mechanics which render technology endogenous.

Economic development is viewed like a process which moves over time to the long run growth.

Endogenous technological change is partial if it is applied to a little part of the whole country's firms. Otherwise, if it is applied to all the firms of the whole country, the endogenous technological change is complete. Technological change concept is associated to country's opening degree. Therefore, firm and country are the main engines of growth and development. Firm's behavior and country's situation in regard to the rest of the world determinate demand supply of goods though effective demand concept of Keynes (1936).

The analysis is not limited to growth literature only. It is also based on development economics theory. The

Chapitre N° 1

The Preliminary Analysis

1 PRESENTATION

The analysis is conducted on the basis of Romer (1990) results, a growth model where technology is endogenous i.e technological change results from the decisions of the agents who maximize their profits. The adaptation of this model to our study means that, technology character of inputs of production can be partially or completely "endogenous". The entrepreneur's behavior and market size are the mechanics which render technology endogenous.

Economic development is viewed like a process which moves over time to the long run growth.

Endogenous technological change is partial if it is applied to a little part of the whole country's firms. Otherwise, if it is applied to all the firms of the whole country, the endogenous technological change is complete. Technological change concept is associated to country's opening degree. Therefore, firm and country are the main engines of growth and development. Firm's behavior and country's situation in regard to the rest of the world determinate demand supply of goods though effective demand concept of Keynes (1936).

The analysis is not limited to growth literature only. It is also based on development economics theory. The description of the development process is based on *Rostow* (1960) and the analytical tools used belong to the growth theory. *Rostow* (1960) views development such as a process with several stages over time. Moreover, international trade theory used is initiated by *Ricardo (1817)* on the basis of comparative advantages in international trade. Rather than assuming preliminary advantages of the country in a given resources such as raw materials in the concern of poor countries, the comparative advantages concept used here is associated to creative skills based on new technology understanding through investments in R&D and in human capital accumulation in order to be absorbed in production sector.

The book contains four chapters linked the one to the others where total chapters constitutes the whole theory. The understanding of the theory requires the follow of its developments along the book.

The first chapter is the presentation of the literature of development economics in order to show what can be learned and how to use information.

The second chapter introduces to *partial* endogenous technological change concept.

The third chapter completes the theory and introduces to *complete* endogenous technological change. It also gives the first results of global economic dynamics behavior of poor countries.

Finally, chapter 4 closes the book and evaluates *complete* endogenous technological change notion because chap 3 main result highlights that, economic development is a random dynamics system with nine possible solutions, the long run path is hard to reach. Chapter 4 is a deeper study of chapter 3 methodology and finds that, global economic dynamics admits a unique equilibrium. Therefore, development dynamics is no more a random process. Finally, a unique equilibrium highlights the mechanics of economic development.

Before the presentation of the analysis, it is useful to introduce to fundamental economic modeling process in order to see later on how to deal with it. The first step aim is to view the literature in order to see how the subject is analyzed. It is also useful to know what questions have already been raised and investigated in order to look for a new approach of the question i.e non examined aspects of the problem by the literature. The goal is to provide a valuable addition to economic research and to justify the usefulness of the study to do. This compulsory step aim is to make sure of the novelty of the study proposed especially in terms of foundations more than on tools used. Because research in economics implies questions to deal with, more than equations to solve and/ or tools to provide. If it is the case i.e tools are introduced, then their aim must necessary be to improve the understanding of a given problem. Thus, key remains on theoretical foundations to provide in order to view the problem with fresher eyes. Appropriate questions are welcome and may be asked on the basis of results already known for it to be more a continuous process than a break point in regard to the literature of the analysis.

The analysis of this book improves development economics literature on the basis of Romer (1990). Theoretical foundations provided are based on growth literature and specifically on Romer (1990) as well as development economics which makes sense since African countries still under developed.

Theoretical foundations of chapters 2 up to 4 aims are the rise of standard development theory through conventional frameworks.

Standard development economics can be understood through growth theory, the one we're going to use in order to understand the economics phenomena.

Growth theory methodology can be applied to almost all the questions someone needs to understand and specifically, development.

At its initiation with Lewis (1954), Rostow (1960), Hirschman (1958), Roseinstein-Rodan (1943) for example, standard theory of development economics wanted to have its own methodological process. Unfortunately, economists were unable to conduct the analysis with well specified methodology, indeed the theory fall in the mid 1970s [Krugman (1994)].

Consequently, to study development economics in this book several steps are used where the first step is variables provision through three studies which are: Easterly, Pritchett and the World Bank. Those analysis results support the theory of chapters 2 up to 4 of this current book. Therefore, theoretical foundations of development economics require several basis studies to be conducted. Each step and analysis provided has a well specific role in the build of the theory. Literature as a great value in the analysis conducted, there must be established a link among them. The link established between the literature of development economics and the book's analysis gives breath to the study and increases its originality.

The variables selection step serves as a basis of the theoretical analysis to do. The literature serves as a basis of the study. It can be supported both by empirical and theoretical studies. The literature chosen is based on empirical works, as we've seen it, development economics is actually mostly visited by both empirical and survey works in contrast to macroeconomic model built here.

2   THE LITERATURE OF THE MODEL

Development economics is an economic field which study poor countries growth absence. It focuses on the determinants of poverty as well as of under development in order to recommend the best economic policy able to improve poor countries capability to realize positive growth rates.

Standard development theory was initiated in 1940s by Roseinstein-rodan (1943), the theory rapidly unraveled to the point where in the mid 1970s, it became incomprehensible. Since the mid 1970s, economists have broken through this barrier in a number of fields: international trade, economic growth and finally, development. Therefore, examples provided in first analysis step are based on empirical studies. First step aim is to show how development studies raised question and generate research question from the literature.

2.1 Presentation of the literature of the analysis

2.1.1 Willaim Easterly work

Easterly work' aim is to analyze empirically Union Nations and the British commission for Africa's development goal in 2005 i.e

Massive investments combination may lead African economies to get out of poverty trap

The author tests the above proposition using growth rates regressions. In parallel, he tests poverty trap existence. This question has been already studied by Roseinstein-rodan (1943) and Azariadis-Drazen (1990). Eastely makes stationary tests of per-capita growth rate, poverty trap assumption is validate if *per-capita income log of the poor countries is stationary* if the hypothesis is not validate then, *per-capita growth rates fluctuates randomly to its average level.*

The stationary test is based on comparison of hypothesis H_0 against hypothesis H_1 i.e

H_0={*per-capita income log is stationary*} against

H_1={ *per-capita income log is not stationary*}

Regression results (see the following array) explain growth rate by initial income and democracy indicators of politic institutions.

Poverty trap existence assumption is not retained because results found stipulate that:

Few countries have achieved a per-capita growth rate inside the range [-0.5; 0,5] in the period 1950-2000 and per-capita income log is not stationary.

Indeed, none country among those included in the sample is kept in a poverty trap because long run absence of per-capita growth is not observed along the period studied.

Moreover, development aid's impact on investment and growth is not clear, foreign aid is not a take-off fundamental tool. In contrast, political institutions are.

Testing the poverty trap for long periods

Per capita growth for:	1950-2001	1950-75	1975-2001	1980-2001	1985-2001
Poorest fifth at beginning of period indicated	1.6%	1.9%	0.8%	0.5%*	0.2%*
All others	1.7%	2.5%**	1.1%	0.9%	1.3%**
Reject stationary income for poorest fifth	Yes	Yes	Yes	Yes	Yes
Fail to reject nonstationary income for poorest fifth	Yes	Yes	Yes	Yes	Yes

*Poorest fifth not statistically distinguishable from zero
**All others's growth statistically distinguishable from poorest fifth
Sample: 137 countries. Statistical tests exclude 12 transition economies and Gulf oil states

2.1.2 The World Bank analysis

The following ascertainment:

Average per-capita income of 20 richest countries is 37 times higher than average income of 20 poorest countries

Relative income ratio of poorest countries is characterized such that:

-Take-off is a successive continuous growth regimes followed by a continuous successive positive growth regimes.

Per-capita growth rate is zero if we have: $-0.5 \leq g \leq 0.5$

Per-capita growth rate is positive and stable since $g > 1.5$

The following chart characterizes development

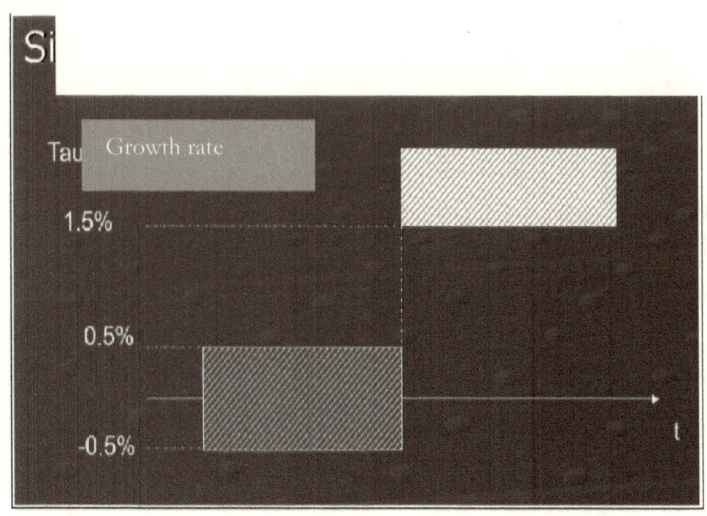

Consequently, only South Eastern Asia satisfies development definition given above. Latin America and Caribbean countries knew prior take-off during the period 1870-1923

2.1.3 Pritchett (1996)

Pritchett makes regressions in order to explain per-capita growth rates by initial income as well as democracy and political institutions indexes.

The results found are summarized in the following array. The explanation power is not clear.

In regard to results viewed, fundamental notions of development economics are *poverty, under development* as well as *political institutions*.

The main question is *to explain growth process foundations in poor countries.*

Growth is absents, the aim of the study is to analyze development through a formal model in order to evidence the mechanics able to explain development.

OLS Regressions for Divergence Big Time: Growth Per Capita on Initial Income and Democracy Average in the Long Run								
	Growth Rate 1820-2001				Growth Rate 1870-2001			
Regression	(1)	(2)	(3)	(4)	(1)	(2)	(3)	(4)
Initial income	0.00468	0.00335	0.00113	0.00036	0.00181	0.00031	-0.00388	-0.00265
	3.8	2.32	0.84	0.24	1.77	0.21	-1.90	-1.58
Democracy average Polity IV		0.00037	0.00081			0.00041	0.00110	
		1.96	5.76			1.87	3.76	
Democracy average Polity IV corrected for colonies				0.00083				0.00099
				4.7				3.93
Constant	-0.01770	-0.01078	0.00260	0.00785	0.00305	0.01131	0.03804	0.02989
	-2.11	-1.16	0.29	0.83	0.42	1.17	2.81	2.71
# observations	52	51	32	51	63	62	39	62
R-squared	0.169	0.258	0.633	0.386	0.040	0.102	0.333	0.208

According to literature, financial support of economic policy based on foreign aid is not efficient enough to contribute strongly to poor countries development goal.

Consequently, the analysis of the following chapters doesn't use foreign aid as a development tool. Tools selected for development and poverty eradication over time are based on self development policy. Economic phenomenon of interest is *theoretical development of growth through market size increase* in order to eradicate poverty, under development or growth absence in poor economies. We find that, development is a random dynamic process with several stages which are under development, take-off and development.

Chapter N° 2

Partial endogenous technological change

1 DEFINITIONS

According to economic growth literature, a given country is in development if poverty is high and growth is low. A given country is developed if poverty is neutral and/ or low as well as growth high [Azariadis-Drazen (1990)].

When knowledge financial support is private, externalities don't exist. In contrast, public knowledge financial support creates externalities [Lucas (1988), Chen (2006, 2008)].

Therefore knowledge is a monotone increasing function and decreasing function of financial support. The intercept of public and private financial support of knowledge defines knowledge threshold corresponding to the world average level, h^* which differentiates developed and developing countries in terms of knowledge.

More precisely, $h_t \geq \hat{h}$ means that, the economy is opened and provides great knowledge externalities through innovations in intermediate goods through R&D investments.

When current knowledge level h_t is established such that $h^* \leq h_t < \hat{h}$, then economy is only partially opened and innovations in technological goods are averagely high.

In contrast, when current knowledge level is such that $0<h_t<h^*$, the economy is under developed and kept in a poverty trap, technology is not evocated.

The following models economic situation of a little country which aim is to get developed in increasing is technological level. The basic model of the analysis is Romer (1990) results as well as Pritchett, Easterly and the World Bank introduced earlier in the analysis. The study mainly focuses on the endogenous character of technology. The methodology is a step by step process to highlight economic model principles based on growth theory which uses Ramsey (1928), Cass (1965), Koopmans (1965) mathematical approaches in the Solow (1956) framework.

2 THE ANALYTIC METHODOLOGY

Let a little opened economy inside which a low tech firm produces artisanal goods and a high tech firm produces manufactured goods of the same homogenous consumption good in competition.

At time t high tech firms have an average per-capita human capital level h_t in contrast to low tech firm which per-capita human capital level is $h_t^0 < h_t$.

The aim of high tech firm is to be as close as possible to world average human capital level, h^* in order to increase market size through international exchange of goods with developed country in international market. High tech firm wants to increase labor skills in order to increase economic competitiveness.

In parallel, low tech firm keeps his development level constant in partial technological change regime. Low tech firm's production requires discarded technology only.

High tech firm' aim is to get in international exchange market through a temporal investment perspective as already said. Therefore, high tech firm is endowed with a total time normalized to 1 where *1-e$_t$* is per-capita time spent by a given worker of the firm in good production and the remaining time *e$_t$* is spent in knowledge acquisition through learning by doing in order to understand the developed country's technology. New knowledge comes from developed country which is a leader in high tech goods. But understanding of new knowledge needs sufficient endowment and sufficient skill to absorb new technology in good production.

Low tech firm agent allocates *1-u_t* time in good production and the rest u_t in learning. At the end of the period, firms have significant human capital differences due both to knowledge and human capital accumulation increases.

In this first part we assume that, high tech firms invest in knowledge and low tech firms don't invest in knowledge. High tech firm increases knowledge through international exchange of goods with the rich country B with an open of the country at a degree *p*.

Opening degree is partial if *p*ε*]0, 1[*, then per-capita knowledge is h_t such that $h^* \leq h_t < \hat{h}$.

In contrast, when opening degree is complete i.e $p=1$ then $h_t \geqslant \hat{h}$.

Developing country's exchange terms with the developed country depend on $\theta \varepsilon]0, 1]$ such that, firms are indifferent to national and foreign goods if $0<\theta<1$. When $\theta>1$, foreign goods are preferred by the developing country's firms.

Production functions of high and of low tech firms depend on technology preference choices, $h_{t+1}{}^o$ and h_{t+1}.

Intermediate goods acquisitions are evaluated in terms of parameters p and θ. Production functions of the high and the low tech sectors of production are respectively expressed such that:

$$F_t^H = \ln(1-e_t) + \beta^h \left[(1-p)\ln(w_t^A h_{t+1}) + p \ln(w_t^B h_{t+1})\right]$$
(2.1)

$$F_t^L = \ln(1-u_t) + \bar{\beta}^h Ln\left(w_t^{0,A} h_{t+1}^0\right) \qquad (2.2)$$

(β^i)$_i$ is the discount rate, $\theta \succ 0$ highlights high tech firm's preference between national and foreign goods i.e from countries A or B.

The variables w_t^A and w_t^B are earns of high tech firms on intermediate goods from the countries A and B respectively.

Knowledge is a universal good which accumulates uniformly in the both countries.

In knowledge terms the differences between A and B result from the investment differentials in R&D. The law of motion of the high and the low tech sectors' knowledge are respectively such that:

$$h_{t+1} = \phi e_t^\gamma h_t^\delta \qquad (2.3)$$

$$h_{t+1}^0 = \mu(u_t, h_t^0) \qquad (2.4)$$

$\gamma+\delta=1$ for knowledge to move at a constant rate and the susbstituability between time spent in training and in current knowledge be ensured,

φ and μ are respective productivities of the high and the low tech sectors,

$\gamma, \delta \ \varepsilon(0,1)$ are elasticities of the R&D training and of the high tech knowledge accumulation.

The decision to invest in knowledge accumulation e_t of the firms which are willing to engage in international exchange of intermediate goods is obtained through resolution of production function after introducing knowledge accumulation inside.

Setting to zero the derivative in respect to e_t, determinate equilibrium time devoted to high tech knowledge understanding $e_t(p)^*$ i.e

$$e_t(p)^* = \frac{\gamma\beta^h[1+(\theta-1)p]}{1+\gamma\beta^h[1+(\theta-1)p]} \qquad (2.5)$$

Assuming $\theta > 1$ then movements of p increase high tech firm incentives to invest in knowledge understanding, finally, through decision to invest in knowledge, technology becomes endogenous. This finding is due to endogenous growth literature [Romer (1986), Lucas (1988)] which began in the mid 1980s and explains growth mechanics in order to differentiate countries in development economics level terms. In contrast, Solow (1956) is an exogenous technological change model. In new models, poor countries and the rich countries are not the same in the long run [Romer (1986), Lucas (1988), Azariadis-Drazen (1990)].

Applying previous methodology to low tech firms, equilibrium time spent learning is such that

$$u_t^* = 1/1+\beta^{\bar{h}} \qquad (2.6)$$

Equation (2.6) differs of equation (2.5) in a sense that, it doesn't depend on the economic development mechanics of international exchange. It only depends on the discount rate. Indeed technological change is exogenous like in neoclassical growth model of Solow (1956) where decision made is not clear and thus, is an ad-hoc formula.

In expect results perspective, production remains without explanation factors because the decision related to low tech sector of production doesn't explain sources of observed benefits highlighted by the data. This is due to the fact that, data don't have an impact on production function. Therefore, low tech sector of production highlights Solow (1956) model where it is impossible to undertake development economics policy. In the long run, poor countries grow faster than rich countries because of the hypothesis of decreasing marginal returns of capital stock. Poor and rich countries converge to the same long run locus, thus there aren't theoretical foundations to distinguish poor to rich countries.

Endogenous growth models reject the capital stock marginal decreasing returns hypothesis in order to establish theoretical foundations which distinguish poor to rich countries anytime and anywhere. Initiated by

Romer (1986) and Lucas (1988), endogenous growth theory introduces increasing returns in the production of knowledge to distinguish the countries [Romer (1986)]. Lucas (1988) introduces human capital accumulation in the education sector to do the same thing. Azariadis-Drazen (1990) considers empirical evidence that, threshold externalities are associated with human capital accumulation, rapid growth cannot occur without relatively overqualified labor. That is, without a *high level of human investment or knowledge relative to per-capita income,* an economy may generate multiple stable stationary states. If the economy exhibits bifurcations at critical points for different parameter values, it is called *the threshold effects.* They are radical differences in dynamic behavior arising from local variations in social returns to scale. Such bifurcations may result from the technical features of the accumulation process in an economy with both physical and human capital. Indeed, human capital accumulation thresholds create externalities.

We apply those results to high tech firms of a little country. A parallel can be done inside the same country with low tech firms such that differences which prevail result from development levels due to investment differentials.

3 DETERMINATION OF KNOWLEDGE DYNAMICS

For simplicity, developing country's variables are not indexed yet because the developed country is out of the analysis at the beginning.

Low tech firm technology is exogenous which means that, the acquisition of technology is not linked to development economics mechanics based on market size increase. Labor force is unskilled, firm's path is under developed expressed by dynamics $\varphi_h^0(0,t,h_t^0) = h_{t+1}^0$ ∀t, where

$$h_{t+1}^0 = \mu(1/1+\beta^{\bar{h}})h_t^0 \qquad (3.1)$$

Exogenous character of technology is linked to before the mid 1980s growth models where sources of growth are not explained.

In parallel, high tech firm describes a dynamic process which varies over time. Therefore firms face the following situation at *t* such that:

$0 \leq t < t_0$ at initial time, high tech average per-capita knowledge, h_t is such that $0 < h_t < h^*$. Those firms work in the same environment as low tech firms which per-capita human capital level still h_t^0 inside the range $[0, h_t[$. Opening rate of the both firms at initial time is $p=0$ which means that, the country is closed in regard both to international exchange of final goods and equipment or intermediate goods necessary to produce new final goods. High tech goods technology and low tech goods technology are exogenous at initial time.

Under developed dynamics of the high tech firm is $\varphi_h(0, t, h_t) = h_{t+1}^1$ i.e

$$h_{t+1}^1 = \phi \left[\frac{\gamma \beta^h}{1 + \gamma \beta^h} \right]^\gamma h_t^\delta \qquad (3.2)$$

The dynamics doesn't depend on θ because the country is closed and the agents' human capital level is too low to be able to absorb the developed country's technology. Under development results from low incentives to invest in R&D [Romer (1990)] which retains the economy in a poverty trap [Romer (1986), Lucas (1988), Azariadis-Drazen (1990)]. Therefore there is necessarily knowledge externalities absence otherwise, because knowledge can't be kept secret [Romer (1990)], if there were some, the economic dynamics won't be kept in a poverty trap.

-At t such that $t_0 \leq t < T$, per-capita knowledge h_t increases and holds such that $h^* \leq h_t < \hat{h}$, developing country opens partially to international exchange i.e only for high tech production sector, for a fraction p where $0 < p < 1$. Therefore, knowledge dynamics gets in the take-off regime $\rho_h(p,t,h_t) = h_{t+1}^2$ which moves such that:

$$h_{t+1}^2 = \phi \left[\frac{\gamma \beta^h [1 + (\theta-1)p]}{1 + \gamma \beta^h [1 + (\theta-1)p]} \right]^\gamma h_t^\delta \qquad (3.3)$$

$0 < \theta \leq 1$

For instance, high tech firm is indifferent between national and foreign goods, when $t_0 \leq t < T$, there are low knowledge externalities because $0 < p < 1$. Technology is partially endogenous because the opening degree between the countries A and B is limited. Low tech firm doesn't participate to the international exchange market.

Finally when $t \geq T$, average current per-capita knowledge of the high tech sector is $h_t \succ \hat{h}$, developing country opens fully to the international exchange market. Therefore $p=1$ and $\theta \succ 1$, per-capita knowledge dynamics $\rho_h(1,T,h_t) = h_{t+1}^3$ gets in development stage, moves such as

$$h_{t+1}^3 = \phi \left[\frac{\gamma \beta^h \theta}{1 + \gamma \beta^h \theta} \right]^\gamma h_t^\delta \qquad (3.4)$$

this case highlights « strong knowledge externalities » between countries B i.e developed country and A i.e developing country. Technology is "partially" endogenous. The increase of knowledge dynamics needs incentives to invest in R&D as it is empirically observed for high technological level countries.

4 MACROECONOMICS INTERPRETATION OF THE ANALYSIS

The dynamics law of motion at initial time i.e the under development dynamics previously introduced $\varphi_h(0,t_0,h_t)=h^1_{t+1}$ doesn't depend on θ and p. In contrast

$$\varphi_h(p,t,h_t)=h^2_{t+1} \text{ and}$$

$$\varphi_h(1,T,h_t)=h^3_{t+1}$$

depend on θ and p respectively such that $0<p<1$ and $0<\theta<1$ as well as $p=1$ and $\theta>1$

We assume in this first part that, low tech firm doesn't beneficiate of knowledge externalities in a direct way. It may be true indirectly if they use recent discarded technologies previously used in the high tech sector until the happening of a new innovation.

Economic system movements result from the average per-capita knowledge h_t movements due to international opening measured by p and θ. Increase in p opens the country to international exchange of high quality goods in a bilateral relation. This connection with the developed country necessitates incentives to invest in R&D in order to adapt to international concept as well as to absorb new knowledge in production process [Eicher (1996)]. Thus $0<\theta\leq1$ measures the importance of international trade between rich and poor countries, when $\theta=1$, bilateral opening is complete. If the creative/destructive hypothesis [Schumpeter (1942)] is adopted, then there exist knowledge externalities at both the high tech and the low tech production sectors. Otherwise, if this hypothesis is excluded then, the high tech firm keeps his equipment for a long time, introduces depreciation rate in order to keep working with the same goods longer. Therefore, high tech discarded equipment doesn't move too fast from one sector to the other like before, there are almost no knowledge externalities.

4.1 Global dynamics of the first stage

When $0 \leq t < t_0$, there exist h_0 such that $h_0 \leq h_t < h^*$. Global dynamics is the sum of per-capita high tech and low tech firms' growth where per-capita dynamics of low tech firm in the first stage doesn't depend on economic development mechanics.

Global dynamics is
$k_{t+1}(h_t) = h_{t+1}/h_t + h_{t+1}/h_t$ i.e

$$k_{t+1}^0(h_t) = \phi\left[\frac{\gamma\beta^h}{1+\gamma\beta^h}\right]^\gamma h_t^{\delta-1} + \mu/1+\beta^{\bar{h}}$$

(4.1)

Therefore global dynamic system of the poor country at the initial period remains kept in a poverty trap with low per-capita knowledge.

Economic system $k_{t+1}(h_t)$ is under developed, converges to its initial low knowledge level i.e $k_{t+1}(h_0)$ because there are none mechanics able to lead the path at a higher level than its initial level h_t where $h_t < h^*$.

4.2 Global dynamics of the system in the second stage

When $t_0 \leq t < T$, global economic dynamics of the second stage, $k_{t+1}{}'(h_t)$ is such that

$$k_{t+1}^1(h_t) = \phi \left[\frac{\gamma \beta^h [1+(\theta-1)p]}{1+\gamma\beta^h[1+(\theta-1)p]} \right]^\gamma h_t^{\delta-1} + \mu/1+\beta^{\bar{h}}$$

(4.2)

When $t_0 \leq t < T$, there exists h such that $h^* \leq h_t < \hat{h}$, per-capita global economic dynamics of poor country converges to average per-capita world global dynamics $k_{t+1}{}^*(h^*)$.

4.3 The global dynamics of the third stage

When $t \geq T$, global economic dynamics of the third stage, $k_{t+1}{}^2(h_t)$ is such that

$$k_{t+1}^2(h_t) = \phi\left[\frac{\gamma\beta^h\theta}{1+\gamma\beta^h\theta}\right]^\gamma h_t^{\delta-1} + \mu/1+\beta^{\bar{h}} \quad (4.3)$$

Average per-capita knowledge, h_t is such that $h_t \geqslant \bar{h}$, the global economic dynamics jumps to average per-capita knowledge of developed countries, $k_{t+1}^B(h_t)$, therefore $k_{t+1}^2(h_t)$ converges to $k_{t+1}^B(h_t)$, consequently, poor country's economic dynamics gets in growth zone.

Finally, result found is based on the existence of θ and technology transfers of developed country's high tech as well as the open of country.

4.4   Synthesis of the results

global economic dynamics is displayed in a *45°* diagram denoted *D(45°)* through which the system evolution follows several situations i.e

$D(45°) \cap \{h_t=h_0\}$ defines take-off locus

$D(45°) \cap \{h_t=h^*\}$ defines development frontier

$D(45°) \cap \{h_t=h\}$ defines growth locus

$D(45°) \cap \{h_t \varepsilon [0,h_0[\}$ defines poverty trap

$D(45°) \cap \{h_t \varepsilon [h_0,h^*[\}$ defines take-off zone

$D(45°) \cap \{h_t \varepsilon [h^*,h[\}$ defines development zone

$D(45°) \cap \{h_t > \hat{h}\}$ defines growth zone (see the following figure)

Development is reached after take-off. Per-capita world average knowledge h^* accelerates economic dynamics to development. The parameter θ induces great variations of per-capita knowledge h which induce increase of the open of the economy. Therefore the firms' dynamics push the economy of a little country to stages of economic development which are development and growth dynamics through world market's mechanics measured by p.

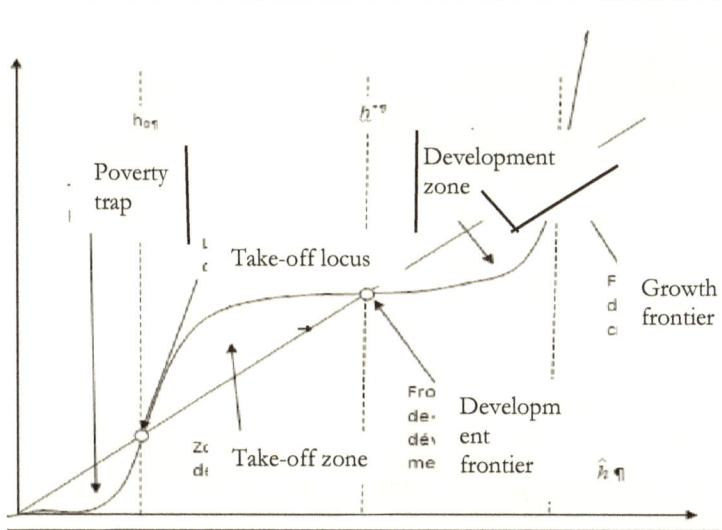

5 GLOBAL DYNAMICS EVOLUTION

5.1 Complete open strategy

-At $t \geq T$ when $h_t^A \geq \hat{h}$, $\theta > 1$ and $p=1$, transitory dynamics velocity evolution from its initial point where the system is under developed to stationary state which is growth frontier, $\varphi_h(1,T,h_t)/\varphi^0 = d_h^2$ where

$$d_{t+1}^2(h_t) = \phi \left[\frac{\gamma \beta^h \theta}{1+\gamma \beta^h \theta} \right]^\gamma h_t^{\delta-1} / [\mu/1+\bar{\beta}^{\bar{h}}]$$

(5.2)

5.2 Partial open strategy

-At $t_0 \leq t < T$ when $h^* \leq h_t^A < \hat{h}$, $0 < \theta < 1$ and $0 < p < 1$, the speed of evolution of transitory take-off path from its initial point where economy is under developed to its stationary state which is development locus is

$$d^1_{t+1}(h_t) = \phi \left[\frac{\gamma \beta^h [1+(\theta-1)p]}{1+\gamma \beta^h [1+(\theta-1)p]} \right]^\gamma h_t^{\delta-1} /[\mu/1+\bar{\beta}^h]$$
(5.3)

5.3 Open absence strategy

At $0 \leq t < t_0$ when $0 < h_t^A < h^*$, $\theta=0$ and $p=0$, the economic system is located at under development stage and its speed toward take-off locus converges to zero i.e

$$d^0_{t+1}(h_t) = \phi \left[\frac{\gamma \beta^h}{1+\gamma \beta^h} \right]^\gamma h_t^{\delta-1} /[\mu/1+\bar{\beta}^h]$$
(5.4)

Therefore, parameters p and θ move economic dynamic from poverty trap to growth zone. Those parameters are the mechanics of economic development because of inducing pushes on the economic system and lead it to transitory zones. This means that, opening and R&D investments increase economic velocity from its initial locus to its long run locus in first step. Therefore, through the speed of convergence, the target reaches its objective and pursuits its acceleration. Finally, it is the movements which allow the economy integrate the international economic market in a progressive way.

Whatever be current economic development regime, without routine knowledge externalities highlighted by q and $\theta^{\bar{h}}$ which are not introduced in the analysis yet, simple task dynamics

$h_{t+1} \stackrel{a}{=} \mu(u_t h_t) = \varphi^0$ remains fix, its convergence speed is close to zero i.e

$$\varphi^0 = \mu/1 + \beta^{\bar{h}}$$
(5.5)

This analysis uses several notions which link production to increasing returns initiated by Smith (1776), considered as the initiator of market based economy conception, associates labor specialization to the nations' capability to create wealth. The idea of increasing returns is crucial to explain sources of long run economic growth. This concept is difficult to formulate explicitly in "dynamic" models.

The use of increasing returns with externalities was limited to models without objective function such in international trade field.

The attempt of Arrow (1962) to take account of increasing returns with externalities in a dynamic model makes him abut on two things:

-the existence of the competitive equilibrium which is effective if the returns are external to the individual firm [Marshall, Young (1928), Hicks (1960), Kaldor (1981)], therefore, the link with the analysis of this book is established through the fact that low tech firms may face increasing returns because they are external to those firms in the industry. Developing country's high tech firms may beneficiate of developed country's high tech firm skills according to Marshall. Inside the same country, this eventuality is effective such when the Schumpeter (1942) destructive-creative hypothesis is adopted.

-the second problem faced by Arrow (1962) comes from the growth models dynamics specificity i.e the existence of optimum and finite of the objective function. When returns are increasing in a dynamic model, consumption function may increase too fast, thus the objective function below the integral may tends to infinity, therefore the optimum doesn't exist. Arrow (1962), Levhari (1966a, 1966b) and Sheshinsky (1967) avoid this problem in making the product to be a function of labor and capital stocks, thus returns are increasing, but they are limited by the labor force growth rate i.e natural growth rate. Consequently, if population growth rate is zero, then the economic growth rate tends to zero too.

Until the mid 1980s, growth theory got discredited because it couldn't solve this dilemma i.e increasing returns in a dynamic model with competitive equilibrium. Romer (1986) solves this dilemma in assuming consumption goods production globally convex and no more concave in function of the stock of knowledge. Social optimum exists because technological research sector exhibits decreasing returns which imply existence of the equilibrium, knowledge growth rate is feasible and allow for a maximum product growth rate. Therefore, production growth rate is monotone increasing over time without exceeding the upper bound. It is a growth model where the competitive equilibrium is with externalities.

In the concern of technical problems raised by Romer (1986), models which have avoided the problem of the finite consumption function have used an instantaneous utility function or have bounded the increasing returns in an optimizing dynamic model [Weitzman (1970), Dixit-Mirrlees-Stern (1975),

Skiba (1978), Majumdar-Mitra (1982, 1983), Dechert-Nishimura (1983)].

The other aspect of the same problem is elaborated by Azariadis-Drazen (1990) which aim is to explain international differences in observed growth rates because those differences are not explained by the Solow (1956) neoclassical growth model. Romer (1986) explains growth differences through the distinction of social production inputs to private production inputs. Lucas (1988) distinguishes public externalities to private externalities created by public incentives to invest in human capital accumulation.

Our model exhibits increasing returns which result from international exchange measured by the parameters, (θ, p). There is not ad-hoc formula due to the non formulation of the decision made by the agents who are willing to maximize their profit like in Romer (1986) and Lucas (1988). Therefore, increasing returns provided by international trade explain development and inequalities both among sectors of production, firms and countries. The model differentiates growth dynamics both of the firms and of the countries. Theoretical foundations of the existence of the developed and the developing countries were established in the mid 1980s models of economic growth.

It is interesting to understand how to change a given developing countries structures. That is the aim of this book to find and prove the existence of one possible way to lift a poor country out of poverty. We do it using fundamental economic modeling methodology.

6 THE STAGES OF ECONOMIC DEVELOPMENT

Economic system is defined by joined per-capita knowledge of both the high and the low tech firms i.e the variables $(h_{t+1}/h_t , h_{t+1}^0/h_t^0)$. Global dynamics moves over time and highlights several stages.

Proposition1: *along the time path (t_0, t, T), global dynamics of the economy admits three development stages i.e*

SDEV is the under development stage where $0 \leq t < t_0$ and $0 \leq h \leq h_o$

DEC is the take-off stage where $t_0 \leq t < T$ and $h_0 < h \leq h^*$

DEV is the development stage where $t \geq T$ and $h_t \geq \hat{h}$

During the *SDEV* stage, under development dynamics of low tech and high tech firms are respectively expressed such as:

$$g^0 = \mu/1 + \beta^{\bar{h}} \tag{6.1}$$

$$g_h^{SDEV} = \phi \left[\frac{\gamma \beta^h}{1 + \gamma \beta^h} \right]^\gamma h_t^{\delta-1} \tag{6.2}$$

At that initial stage, we have $0 < h_t < h^*$, $\theta = 0$ and $0 \leq h^0_t < h^{0,*}$ $\forall$ $0 \leq t < t_0$

economic dynamics of the *DEC* stage is

$$g_h^{DEC}(h_t) = \phi \left[\frac{\gamma \beta^h [1 + (\theta-1)p]}{1 + \gamma \beta^h [1 + (\theta-1)p]} \right]^\gamma h_t^{\delta-1} \tag{6.3}$$

Where

$h^* \leq h_t < \hat{h}$, $0 < \theta < 1$ and $0 \leq h^0_t < h^{0,*}$ $\forall$ $t_0 \leq t < T$

economic dynamics of the *DEV* stage is

$$g_h^{DEV} = \phi \left[\frac{\gamma \beta^h \theta}{1+\gamma \beta^h \theta} \right]^\gamma h_t^{\delta-1} \qquad (6.4)$$

Where

$h \geqslant h$, $\theta > 1$ and $0 \leq h^0 < h^{0,*}$ $\forall t \geqslant T$

Therefore, $g_h^{SDEV} < g_h^{DEC} < g_h^{DEV}$.

Along the three economics development stages crossed by the dynamics, the low tech dynamics stays at the same locus i.e it remains under developed (see the figure).

Consequently, high tech developed country's technology acquisition push developing country's economic dynamics. But the analysis of under development of productive capacities can't be conducted without poverty because they are intimately linked. In parallel, poverty can't be understood without taking account of low tech firms' behavior because they generate local poverty, acts on population and create also global poverty on the economy, thus explains poverty trap.

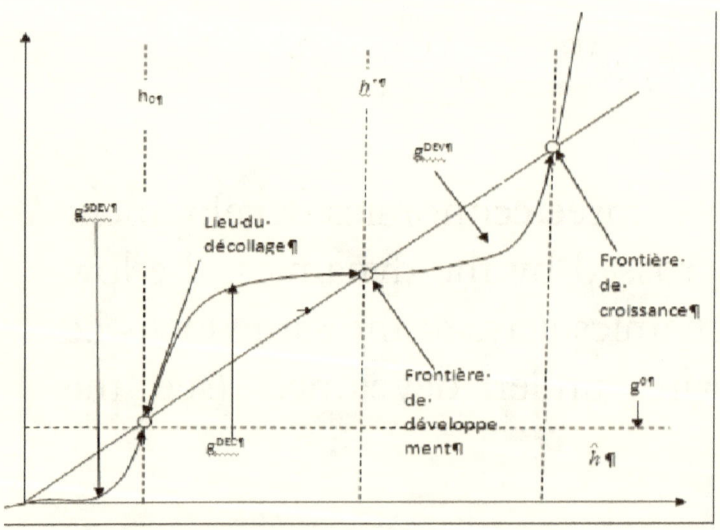

As said above, in this first part, the mechanics of economic development of low tech firms are not highlighted by the analysis i.e we don't know yet, the impact of $\bar{\theta}^h$ and q on the economy.

Therefore, concerning those firms the conditions required for poverty reduction can't be highlighted. Inequalities among the firms as well as poverty can be understood through the action on the global firm to improve competitiveness

Next chapter introduces $\bar{\theta^h}$ and q to study its impact on economic dynamic as well as its capability to converge to long run in order to reduce poverty.

According to above figure, per-capita dynamics converges to successive stages over time. This result opens again the international trade debate. It validates the fact that, international trade is not a game which sum equals zero. This analysis shows a generalized Ricardian law where rather than factors endowments, it deals with international markets size increase through knowledge incorporated in goods. Knowledge externalities or more generally, technology transfers [Bouccekine et al], provide human capital positive externalities [Lucas (1988)].

-For a fixed t, the analysis is static assimilates to following facts:

Agents endowed with $h_t \geq \hat{h}$ when $\theta > 1$ may be engineers or professors.

Agents endowed with $h^* \leq h < \hat{h}$ when $0 < \theta < 1$ may be technicians.

Agents endowed with $0 < h < h^*$ may be worker men.

When $h=0$, agents are not literate i.e agents may be peasants or women.

The study of growth and poverty for a fixed t, assimilates society to several social classes. Therefore, the analysis reduces to a sociological study of poverty and inequalities. The dimension of the analysis is micro, no more macroeconomics.

-When time varies, according to the assumptions made, we deal with a macroeconomics analysis where the dynamic system varies over time, characterized by three stages which are:

$DEV=\{(h_t \geq \hat{h},\ \theta > 1,\ p=1\}$

$DEC=\{h^* \leq h_t < \hat{h},\ 0<p,\theta<1\}$

$SDEV=\{0<h_t<h^*,\ \theta=0,\ p=0\}$

The above classification describes historical dynamic evolution of economy along with technological changes are scientific outcomes like a necessity to join and stay in a large market over time.

The following sections introduce a useful way to maintain the stability of the global system i.e we anticipate an evolution of a system ensuring the equilibrium of the economy. Then the analysis conducted is an equilibrium system preservation analysis in order to find the best long run economic paths.

7 POVERTY AND UNDER DEVELOPMENT

7.1 Poverty

Proposition2: *in a closed economy, the couple of variables of domestic knowledge threshold and poverty rate, (k ,ς(k)) are expressed such that (7.1) and (7.2) i.e*

$$\bar{k} = \mu/1 + \beta^{\bar{h}} \qquad (7.1)$$

$$\varsigma(\bar{k}) = \phi \left[\frac{\gamma \beta^h}{1 + \gamma \beta^h} \right]^{\gamma} h_t^{\delta-1} - \mu/1 + \beta^{\bar{h}} \qquad (7.2)$$

Knowledge threshold, h_{t+1}/h_t^o is the product of the low tech firm's productivity, μ and the intertemporal substitution rate, $1/1+\beta^{\bar{h}}$. This result means that, productivity is a trade-off between current and future income. Equivalently, it means that, reducing firm's productivity today leads to transfer more profits in the future.

Economic system reaches growth frontier since $h_t \geq \hat{h}$ i.e the growth threshold is reached in partial endogenous technology regime. In contrast, per-capita knowledge, h^* is the development threshold. high tech firm accumulates profits which increases its knowledge threshold and leads to higher economic development levels. Setting $\theta=0$, then h^o converges to *its initial level*. Therefore, according to economic literature, economy is kept in a poverty trap because growth generated equals zero. In conformity to previous results, it can be established an approximation between firms endowed with per-capita knowledge level $0<h_t<h^*$ and those endowed of per-capita knowledge $0 \leq h_t^o < h_t$ when $0 \leq t < t_o$ because this fact links poverty to relative and global competition. Nation global poverty threshold $\varsigma(\bar{k})$ can only be defined at under development stage only in order to make knowledge differentials evolution of high and low tech firms balanced i.e $\varsigma(\bar{k})=(h_{t+1}/h_t)-(h_{t+1}^\emptyset/h_t^\emptyset)$ when $0\leq t<t_0$, the following curve describes evolution of poverty with economic development event through economic policy we are presenting.

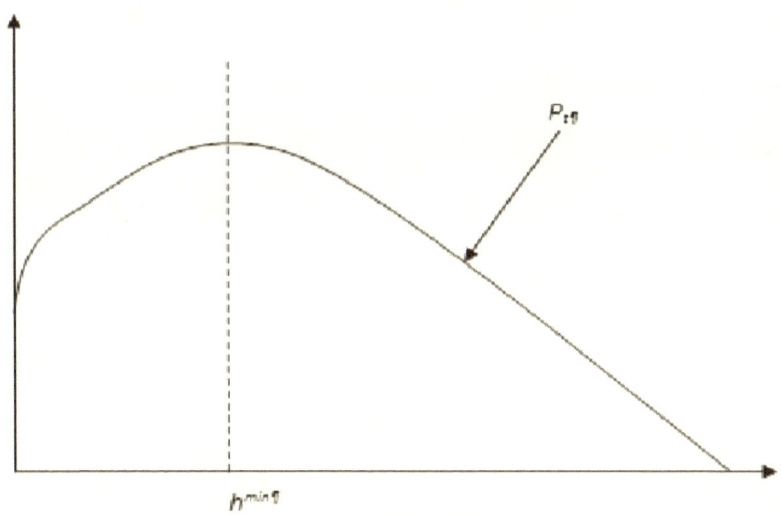

7.2 Analysis of under development and poverty

Minimizing the previous poverty function $\varsigma(\bar{k})$, we determinate average knowledge level which guarantees zero poverty i.e $h^{min}<h^*$ such that h_t^0 converges to h^{min} i.e

$$h^{min} = \left[\frac{\phi(1+\bar{\beta}^h)}{\mu}\left[\frac{\gamma\beta^h}{1+\gamma\beta^h}\right]^\gamma\right]^{1/1-\delta}$$

(7.3)

Therefore, $\varsigma(\bar{k})=0$ if and only if there exists a per-capita minimum threshold h^{min} such that h_0 converges to h^{min} as well as minimum productivity μ^{min} such that μ^0 converges to μ^{min}.

In that way, in a closed economy, convergence of the routine knowledge dynamics to $h^{min}<h^*$ as well as convergence of per-capita low tech

firm's productivity to $\mu^{min} < \mu^*$ are necessary conditions for the poverty dynamics $\varsigma(k)$ to converge to 0. This finding guarantees the firms sufficient power to lift the economy out of poverty trap. Low tech sector technology must increase in order to reach $(h^{min})^{\delta-1} - \mu/1 + \beta^{\bar{h}} = 0$. Then we obtain expression of required productivity to support low tech production sector such that poverty is minimum i.e

$$\mu^{min} = \left[\phi \left[\frac{\gamma \beta^h}{1+\gamma \beta^h} \right]^\gamma \right]^{1/2} \quad (7.4)$$

Rewriting under development dynamics such that poverty is minimum, then we determinate expression of the under development dynamics i.e

$$g_h^{SDEV} = \left[\phi\left[\frac{\gamma\beta^h}{1+\gamma\beta^h}\right]^\gamma\right]^{1/2} / 1+\beta^{\bar{h}} \qquad (7.5)$$

Previous expression means that low tech and high tech production sectors dynamics ratio at initial time where economy is under developed must move at the same constant rate over time.

8 ECONOMIC COMPETITIVENESS

As just viewed above, partial open of country in regard to high tech firm's knowledge without incentives to renew productive engine of low tech firm, create inequalities in firms' productivity and growth. Poverty curve may increase if we don't assume a constant evolution among firm differentials in order to maintain global stability of economy.

To establish control mechanics which ensure constant evolution of the global dynamics, we define the competitiveness. It is differential dynamics evolutions of high and low tech firms in order to know how to control the global dynamics.

8.1 Competitiveness of the development economics

8.1.1 *The analysis*

The gap between low tech and high tech firms' dynamics define inequalities in regard to firm's competitiveness. Then when t⩾T, firms' inequalities in competitiveness, IC_h^{DEV} are expressed such that

$$IC_h^{DEV} = \phi \left[\frac{\gamma \beta^h}{1+\gamma \beta^h} \right]^{\gamma} h_t^{\delta-1} - \mu/1+\beta^{\bar{h}} \quad (8.1)$$

Where $h_t \geqslant \hat{h}$, $\theta > 1$ and $0 \leq h_t^0 < h^{0,*}$ ∀t

It is necessary to control the dynamic system evolution to ensure stability. We need to look for a per-capita knowledge which ensures equilibrium evolution of differential economic dynamics of low and high tech firms. This equilibrium is determinate by $IC_h^{DEV}=0$ which generate a per-capita knowledge level h^{DEV} such that

$$h^{DEV} = \left[\frac{\phi(1+\beta^{\bar{h}})}{\mu} \left[\frac{\gamma \theta \beta^h}{1+\gamma \theta \beta^h} \right]^{\gamma} \right]^{1/1-\delta} \quad (8.2)$$

The above per-capita knowledge level allows the measurement of the evolution gap of the firms' dynamics. Low tech firm's productivity represents the engine of growth must be adjusted in order to stay in the market because of the competition and poverty increase. Therefore, we look for conditions which ensure the economic system equilibrium evolution. To do that, productivity as well as knowledge threshold must be calibrated in order to establish the convergence of h_t^0 to $h^{DEV} \leq h^*$, this condition ensures the poverty curve evolution stability. It is determinate such that $(h^{DEV})^{\delta-1} - \mu/(1+\beta^{\bar{h}})$ grows without bound [Lucas (1988), King-Rebelo (1987)]. It necessitates that the low tech sector productivity μ converges to μ^{DEV} in the full open economy i.e when $t \geq T$ for the economy to remain stable. Full open economy produces sufficient external effects for development to hold as well as poverty to decrease. The external effects depend on environment. To guarantee that to happen, we must have $[(b^{DEV})^{\delta-1} - \mu/(1+\bar{\beta}^h)] = 0$ or the low tech sector productivity must establishes such that

$$\mu^{DEV} = \left[\phi\left[\frac{\gamma\theta\beta^h}{1+\gamma\theta\beta^h}\right]^\gamma\right]^{1/2} \qquad (8.3)$$

Previous equation establishes a link between high and low tech sectors in order to maintain all the firms' activity in the market. Because the model doesn't deal with unemployment, population stock equals labor force stock at each time. Therefore, this relation expresses a necessity for the firms' technology differentials to share the same market. International trade as no impact on the low tech firms productivity. Without prediction control, low tech sector productivity μ will decrease. We need h_t^0 to converge to $h^{DEV}<h^*$ and μ to converge to μ^{DEV} for the system to remain stable. This result assumes the existence of knowledge externalities of high tech to low tech firms. That knowledge inflow assumes adoption of creative-destructive Schumpeterian hypothesis of innovations. This assumption means that, innovations follow a fish law of probability. Therefore innovations are randomly distributed but their coming render the last innovation discarded and let it to the use of the low tech sector. Then knowledge external effects inflow indirectly from the high to the low tech sectors of production. Therefore there exist h^{DEV} and μ^{DEV} which render the low and the high tech sectors of production dynamics grow at the same

rate. Consequently, we determinate the development dynamics such that:

$$g^{DEV} = \left[\phi\left[\frac{\gamma\theta\beta^h}{1+\gamma\theta\beta^h}\right]^\gamma\right]^{1/2} /1+\beta^{\bar{h}} \qquad (8.4)$$

8.2 DEC regime competitiveness

8.2.1 The analysis

In *DEC* regime, inequalities in terms of competitiveness differentials of high and low tech firms, IC_h^{DEC} is defined such that:

$$IC_h^{DEC} = \phi\left[\frac{\gamma\theta\beta^h[1+(\theta-1)p]}{1+\gamma\theta\beta^h[1+(\theta-1)p]}\right]^\gamma h_t^{\delta-1} \; {-\mu/1+\beta^{\bar{h}}}$$

(8.5)

Where $h^* \leq h_t < \hat{h}$, $0 < \theta < 1$ and $t_0 < t < T$

To minimize inequalities in order to prevent poverty like in the previous case, we determinate knowledge threshold which ensures a stable evolution of the economy i.e

$$h^{DEC} = \left[\frac{\phi(1+\bar{\beta}^h)}{\mu} \frac{\gamma \theta \beta^h [1+(\theta-1)p]}{1+\gamma \theta \beta^h [1+(\theta-1)p]} \right]^{\gamma} \right]^{1/1-\delta} h_t^{\delta-1}$$

(8.6)

Opening increases general knowledge and thus increases the economic development level. To ensure the viability of the system, the average productivity must establish such that:

$$\mu^{DEC} = \phi\left(1+\beta^{\bar{h}}\right)\left[\frac{\gamma\theta\beta^{h}[1+(\theta-1)p]}{1+\gamma\theta\beta^{h}[1+(\theta-1)p]}\right]^{\gamma} h_{t}^{\delta-1}$$

(8.7)

In order to make μ converges to μ^{DEC} like in the previous case, the *DEC* or the take-off dynamics is expressed such that

$$g^{DEC} = \phi\left[\frac{\gamma\theta\beta^{h}[1+(\theta-1)p]}{1+\gamma\theta\beta^{h}[1+(\theta-1)p]}\right]^{\gamma} h_{t}^{\delta-1}$$

(8.8)

If R&D investments are too low or equal to zero, then knowledge accumulation externalities created by open economy are unable to boost the economy which remains at its initial locus [Azariadis-Drazen (1990)], economy converges to its initial path [Lucas (1988)] and if poverty was there, economy remains kept in a trap.

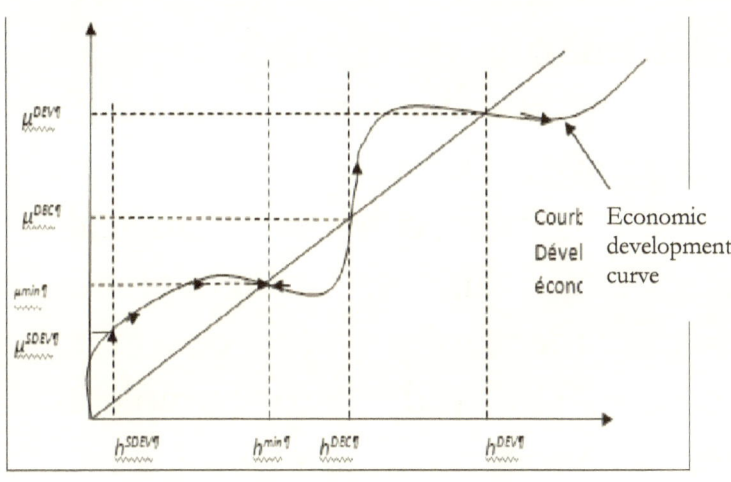

9 CONCLUSION OF THE CHAPTER

Development process modeled above is based on Romer (1990) untitled « exogenous technological change » and Rostow (1960). We wanted to know how to create development through technological change. We knew the growth absence problem of the developing countries through Easterly, Pritchett and the World Bank works which we questioned preliminary. We could determinate the study's area in order to apply the concepts found and the tools to use. The whole reveal that development is created by technological change. The analysis highlighted preliminary mechanics of economic development. The study is not complete because, endogenous technological change doesn't touch all the firms of the country.

Before viewing global analysis dynamics, we introduced crucial notions linking development dynamics to growth concepts. As we've seen the preliminary check highlighted two possible issues of the study which were a micro or a macro level and we've chosen the macro level. Meaning we decided to examine a global study. In that purpose, we used Rostow (1960) development concept such as several stages and we have presented three stages rather than five like he did. But we wanted to present a general equilibrium analysis, thus we had to maintain the economic stability hypothesis which led us look for both per-capita knowledge and associated productivity of the low tech firms in order to converge to the equilibrium path. The study shows that poverty must be slowed for the global equilibrium to hold otherwise the low tech sector may fall into poverty and make our general equilibrium model collapse. In concrete aspect, maintaining viable all the economic system needs an intervention to support the economy. But the study doesn't introduce public policy or development aids for example. It only assumes knowledge positive external effects brought through the Schumpeterian (1942) hypothesis of creative-destructive. If this hypothesis is not under taken, then the study only addresses signals for the economic system prevention to the social planner.

More generally, the analysis concludes to knowledge increase due to the increase of the market in response to R&D investments. Therefore, growth and development are intimately linked to international exchange or market size increase which we call increasing returns [Smith (1776)] generated by inputs endowments in high technology [Ricardo (1817)].

Always in development understanding perspective, analysis generalizes optimization behavior of low tech firms in examining now the case where they invest in appropriate technology through international exchange. Like before, those investments are assumed to increase of their human capital level in order to understand and adapt those technologies in the production sector.

Next chapter examines *complete endogenous technological change* in order to determinate global economic dynamics in the case where all the firms may invest in R&D or not. We find that, global economic dynamics is unstable. The next chapter ends the analysis after the determination of the unique equilibrium through changes of tools used to study profits and growth.

SECOND PART

The Strategy of economic development

Chapter N° 3

Complete Endogenous Technology

1 THE ANALYTICAL METHODOLOGY

To render technological progress completely endogenous, we re-write low tech production function viewed before, such that it contains incentives to invest in new technology i.e new intermediate goods.

In this part, we introduce low tech firms incentives to increase productivity in order to increase competitiveness with the high tech firms.

Production function of low tech firm becomes

$F_t^L =$

$$\ln(1-u_t)+\bar{\beta}^h\left[(1-q)\ln\left(w_t^{0,A}h_{t+1}^{0,A}\right)+q\bar{\theta}^h\ln\left(w_t^{0,B}h_{t+1}^{0,B}\right)\right]$$
(1.1)

$\bar{\beta}^h$ is the discount rate, $\bar{\theta}^h > 0$ highlights technology preferences in regard to national or foreign goods.

Routine knowledge is a universal good which accumulates uniformly in both the developed and the developing countries. The fraction q represents opening degree of the developing country to rich country for high quality low tech goods.

The law of motion of routine knowledge is expressed such that:

$$h_{t+1}^0 = \mu(u_t h_t^0) \qquad (1.2)$$

Where

$\mu\ \varepsilon(0,1)$ is low tech firm's productivity parameter and

h_t^0 is per-capita initial low tech firm's knowledge.

The low tech firm is willing to invest in learning by doing [Arrow (1962), Lucas (1988)]. Therefore, a labor force spends a fraction of time u_t learning in the production process in order to adapt new low tech knowledge (which still new in developing country) in the production sector, remaining time i.e $1-u_t$ is devoted to low tech good production to increase the competitiveness. The equilibrium decision is determinate by time spent learning i.e

$$u_t(q)^* = \beta^{\bar{h}}\left[1+\left(\theta^{\bar{h}}-1\right)q\right]\left[1+\beta^{\bar{h}}\left[1+\left(\theta^{\bar{h}}-1\right)q\right]\right]^{-1}$$
(1.3)

$\theta^{\bar{h}}$ highlights incentives to invest on new intermediate goods of low tech firm in order to improve production.

When $0<\bar{\theta^h}\leq 1$, low tech firm is indifferent between national or foreign goods

When $\bar{\theta^h}>1$, low tech firm likes foreign goods more than national goods

Consequently, $\bar{\theta^h}$ absence means learning by doing incentives absence following Azariadis-Drazen (1990), per-capita knowledge equilibrium threshold of both the low and high techs is establish such that $h_t^{0,A}\leq h_0^*\leq h_t^{0,B}$. Through this distinction, the analysis aim is to study the economic dynamics under incentives to invest in knowledge and its impact on local and global poverty as well as on economic competitiveness under complete endogenous technological change.

2 EVOLUTION OF THE ECONOMIC DYNAMICS

2.1 The first stage dynamics

When $0 \leq h_t^0 < h^*$ at initial time, incentives to invest in learning by doing in order to improve basic knowledge and production process as well as returns, equal to zero. Therefore $q=0$ because productivity and competitiveness are too low for knowledge investments to be conducted. Indeed, low tech firms dynamics in under developed i.e

$\varphi_0(0, h_t^0) = h_{t+1}^{0,0}$ or

$$h_{t+1}^{0,0} = \left[\mu \beta^{\bar{h}} / 1 + \beta^{\bar{h}} \right] h_t^0 \qquad (2.1)$$

2.2 The second stage economic dynamics

When $h^{0,*} \leq h_t^{0,A} < \hat{h}^0$ along the period $t_0 \leq t < T$, opening increases incentives to acquire new knowledge which opens the economy at a degree q where $0<q<1$; Because low tech firm's productivity has increased with new knowledge introduction, low tech firm dynamics is $\varphi_0(q, h_t^0) = h_{t+1}^{0,1}$ i.e

$$h_{t+1}^{0,1} = \left[\mu \beta^{\bar{h}} \left[+ \left(\theta^{\bar{h}} - 1 \right) \right] \left[+ \beta^{\bar{h}} \left[+ \left(\theta^{\bar{h}} - 1 \right) \right] \right]^1 h_t^0$$
(2.2)

Therefore sophisticated developed country's techniques get in low tech sector highlights through the parameter $\theta^{\bar{h}}$. In contrast to previous case, there exist incentives to accumulate knowledge measured by the parameter $0<q<1$, which means indifference in regard to foreign goods compare to national goods.

2.3 The dynamics of the third stage

When $h_t^{0,A} \geqslant h^0$ at $t \geqslant T$, incentives to invest are higher compare to the previous case. Therefore, low tech firm as well as the country are fully open because $q=1$ and $\theta^{\bar{h}}>1$, dynamics is therefore, $\varphi_0(1, h_t) = h_{t+1}^{0,2}$ i.e

$$h_{t+1}^{0,2} = \left[\mu\beta^{\bar{h}}\theta^{\bar{h}}\right]\left[1+\beta^{\bar{h}}\theta^{\bar{h}}\right]^1 h_t^0 \qquad (2.3)$$

In contrast to previous case, incentives to invest in knowledge highlight the existence of complete opening degree for dual exchanges i.e of the country as well as of the firm.

We classify basic knowledge dynamics in different classes like a scale function continuous on all the ranges of the definition and it is increasing function of knowledge levels over time.

In contrast to previous case, incentives to invest highlight a complete opening degree where $\bar{\theta}^h > 1$ and $q=1$.

2.4 The impact of the economic dynamics on the long run

Basic per-capita knowledge dynamics, $h_{t+1}^{0,1} = \varphi_0(q, h_t)$ can't acquire goods outside the country. Denoted $\varphi_0(0, h_t)$ it doesn't depend on $\bar{\theta}^h$

because none alternative investment is engaged.

In contrast to $\varphi_0(1, h_t)$ and $\varphi_0(q, h_t)$ depend on $\theta^{\bar{h}}$ because those dynamics increase low tech sector competitiveness.

Therefore, low tech firm's per-capita knowledge is such that $h_t^0 \gtrless \hat{h}^{0,*}$ and thus, increases of q provide more incentives to invest in production structure where $0 < \theta^{\bar{h}} \leq 1$ highlights the same good preference,

In contrast, $\theta^{\bar{h}} > 1$ highlights high preference for high quality foreign goods.

Therefore we establish the following

2.5 The first stage

Low tech firm at initial period i.e at $0 \leq t < t_0$ faces several scenarios

If $0 \leq h_t \ll h^{0,*}$, there doesn't exist incentives to invest in knowledge in order to improve production and $q = 0$, per-capita routine knowledge dynamics $\varphi_0(0, h_t)$ converges to its initial locus. The system is blocked in the poverty trap with zero growth. The economy is under developed, current economic regime is *SDEV* with zero investment because $\theta^{\bar{h}} = 0$. Therefore, basic knowledge dynamics $\varphi_h(0, h_t)$ is such that :

$$\rho_0(0, h_t^0) = \left[\mu \beta^{\bar{h}} / 1 + \beta^{\bar{h}} \right] h_t^0 \qquad (2.4)$$

2.6 The second regime

When $t_0 \leq t < T$, low tech firm faces $h^{0,*} \leq h_t \ll \hat{h}^0$. Indeed, incentives to invest in knowledge implies an economic opening degree q where $0 < q < 1$. Basic per-capita economic dynamics $\varphi_0(q, h_t)$ converges to average per-capita knowledge of rich country, poor country economic dynamics grows and converges to average per-capita developed country's basic dynamics. Therefore poverty decreases and the take-off happens. In parallel $0 < \theta^{\bar{h}} \leq 1$ because both developed and developing countries goods look like the same in regard to the investors, Indeed, per-capita knowledge h_t^0 converges to $h^{0,*}$.

Economy gets in *DEC* regime through complete endogenous technological change where $h^{0,*} \leq h_t \ll \hat{h}^0$ and $0 < \theta^{\bar{h}} \leq 1$. Basic low tech dynamics of DEC regime $\varphi_0(q, h_t)$ is expressed such that:

$$\varphi_0(q, h_t^0) = \left[\mu \bar{\beta}^{\bar{h}} \left[+ \left(\bar{\theta}^{\bar{h}} - 1 \right) \right] + \bar{\beta}^{\bar{h}} \left[+ \left(\bar{\theta}^{\bar{h}} - 1 \right) \right] \right]^1 h_t^0$$
(2.5)

2.7 The third stage

When $h_t^{0,A} \geq \hat{h}^0$ at $t \geq T$, economy is fully opened, its measures degree is $q=1$. Low tech firm productivity is high, its economic dynamics $\varphi_0(1, h_t)$ jumps on developed country's per-capita dynamics. Therefore, economic development path is in transition to the growth zone. $\bar{\theta}^h > 1$ because low tech firm invests more to improve its production, through external effects, per-capita knowledge becomes $h_t^{0,A} \geq \hat{h}^0$. Therefore, the third stage dynamics is

$$\rho_0\left(1,h_t^0\right)=\left[\mu\bar{\theta}^h\bar{\beta}^h/1+\bar{\theta}^h\bar{\beta}^h\right]h_t^0 \qquad (2.6)$$

Finally, we establish the following inequality

$\varphi_0(0,h_t) < \varphi_0(q,h_t) < \varphi_0(1,h_t)$

Development economics process is a scale function with several stages

Note that, the analysis proposed offers two possible views of the phenomenon, development and inequality. When time is fixed, social classes are not equally distributed and when time moves, the economy is a process through which we look for the long run convergence.

2.8 Determination of the dynamic systems of the economy

Knowledge dynamics of low tech firms in per-capita is expresses such that, $g_h = h_{t+1}°/h_t^0$

Proposition : *low tech dynamics crosses three stages in order to reach its long run growth in the context of endogenous technological change. Those three regimes are: SDEV, DEV and DEC expressed such that:*

$$g_{\bar{h}}^{DEV} = \left[\mu \bar{\theta}^{\bar{h}} \bar{\beta}^{\bar{h}} / 1 + \bar{\theta}^{\bar{h}} \bar{\beta}^{\bar{h}} \right] \quad (2.7)$$

$$g_{\bar{h}}^{DEC} = \left[\mu \bar{\beta}^{\bar{h}} \left[1 + \left(\bar{\theta}^{\bar{h}} - 1 \right) \right] \right] \left[1 + \bar{\beta}^{\bar{h}} \left[1 + \left(\bar{\theta}^{\bar{h}} - 1 \right) \right] \right]^{-1} \quad (2.8)$$

$$g_{\bar{h}}^{SD} = \left[\mu \bar{\beta}^{\bar{h}} / 1 + \bar{\beta}^{\bar{h}} \right] \quad (2.9)$$

It can be seen that the differences between under development economic dynamics and development economic dynamics is $\bar{\theta^h}$ and q existences, the development economics parameters.

3 THE GLOBAL DYNAMICS

Proposition: *global dynamic system is the sum of low tech and high tech dynamics, it defines 9 possible dynamic paths, $(g_{ij})_{1 \leq i,j \leq 3}$ that the economy may take over time i.e*

$$g_{11} = \mu/(1+\bar{\beta^h}) + \left[\phi\left[\frac{\gamma\theta\beta^h}{1+\gamma\theta\beta^h}\right]^\gamma\right]^{1/2} /1+\bar{\beta^h}$$
(3.1)

$$g_{12} = \mu/(1+\bar{\beta^h}) + \phi\left[\frac{\gamma\theta\beta^h[1+(\theta-1)p]}{1+\gamma\theta\beta^h[1+(\theta-1)p]}\right]^\gamma$$
(3.2)

$$g_{13} = \mu/(1+\beta^{\bar{h}}) + \left[\phi\left[\frac{\gamma\theta\beta^h}{1+\gamma\theta\beta^h}\right]^{\gamma}\right]^{1/2} /1+\beta^{\bar{h}}$$
(3.3)

$$g_{21} = \left[\mu\beta^{\bar{h}}\left[+\left(\theta^{\bar{h}}-1\right)y\right]\left[+\beta^{\bar{h}}\left[+\left(\theta^{\bar{h}}-1\right)y\right]\right]^{1} + \left[\phi\left[\frac{\gamma\theta\beta^h}{1+\gamma\theta\beta^h}\right]^{\gamma}\right]^{1/2} /1+\beta^{\bar{h}}$$
(3.4)

$$g_{22} = \left[\mu\beta^{\bar{h}}\left[+\left(\theta^{\bar{h}}-1\right)y\right]\left[+\beta^{\bar{h}}\left[+\left(\theta^{\bar{h}}-1\right)y\right]\right]^{1} + \phi\left[\frac{\gamma\theta\beta^h[1+(\theta-1)p]}{1+\gamma\theta\beta^h[1+(\theta-1)p]}\right]^{\gamma}$$
(3.5)

$$g_{23} = \left[\mu\beta^{\bar{h}}\left[+\left(\theta^{\bar{h}}-1\right)y\right]\left[+\beta^{\bar{h}}\left[+\left(\theta^{\bar{h}}-1\right)y\right]\right]^{1} + \left[\phi\left[\frac{\gamma\theta\beta^h}{1+\gamma\theta\beta^h}\right]^{\gamma}\right]^{1/2} /1+\beta^{\bar{h}}$$
(3.6)

$$g_{31} = \lfloor\mu\bar{\theta}^h\bar{\beta}^h/1+\bar{\theta}^h\bar{\beta}^h\rfloor_{-} + \left[\phi\left[\frac{\gamma\theta\beta^h}{1+\gamma\theta\beta^h}\right]^\gamma\right]^{1/2} /1+\bar{\beta}^h$$
(3.7)

$$g_{32} = \lfloor\mu\bar{\theta}^h\bar{\beta}^h/1+\bar{\theta}^h\bar{\beta}^h\rfloor_{-}$$
$$+ \phi\left[\frac{\gamma\theta\beta^h[1+(\theta-1)p]}{1+\gamma\theta\beta^h[1+(\theta-1)p]}\right]^\gamma$$
(3.8)

$$g_{33} = \lfloor\mu\bar{\theta}^h\bar{\beta}^h/1+\bar{\theta}^h\bar{\beta}^h\rfloor_{-} + \lfloor\mu\bar{\theta}^h\bar{\beta}^h/1+\bar{\theta}^h\bar{\beta}^h\rfloor_{-}$$
(3.9)

In the previous chapter, we defined dynamics of high tech sector in the three regimes. Now, we join them those of low tech firms to constitute global dynamics of poor economy.

Therefore, the 3x3 matrix obtained establishes nine possible trajectories of the economy over time that we represent in the following array:

	g_h^{SDEV}	g_h^{DEC}	g_h^{DEV}
g_h^{SDEV}	g_{11}	g_{12}	g_{13}
g_h^{DEC}	g_{21}	g_{22}	g_{23}
g_h^{DEV}	g_{31}	g_{32}	g_{33}

The different configurations correspond to the following contexts

$g_{11}=(g_h^{SDEV} \cap g_h^{SDEV})$ means that the economy is kept in under development

$g_{12}=(g_h^{SDEV} \cap g_h^{DEC})$ means that the low tech firm is kept in under development whereas the high tech firm faces take-off

$g_{13}=(g_h^{SDEV} \cap g_h^{DEV})$ means that the low tech firm is under developed but the high tech firm is developed

$g_{21}=(g_h^{DEC} \cap g_h^{SDEV})$ means that the low tech firm faces take-off whereas the high tech firm is under developed

$g_{22}=(g_h^{DEC} \cap g_h^{DEC})$ means that the low tech firm and the high tech firm are facing take-off

$g_{23}=(g_h^{DEC} \cap g_h^{DEV})$ means that the low tech firm is facing take-off whereas the high tech firm is getting development

$g_{31}=(g_h^{DEV} \cap g_h^{SDEV})$ means that the low tech firm is getting developed whereas the high tech firm is under developed

$g_{32}=(g_h^{DEV} \cap g_h^{DEC})$ means that the low tech firm is getting developed whereas the high tech firm is facing take-off

$g_{33}=(g_h^{DEV} \cap g_h^{DEV})$ means that the low tech firm is getting developed and the high-tech firm is facing the same thing

We determinate expressions of global dynamics highlight by the above proposition. To understand the link between the analysis and its basic literature, it is interesting to clarify the technological change concept and its advances in the literature. The departure point is the presentation of technological progress by the scale factor, A in the production function of the exogenous technological change

---

[1] K is physical capital stock, L is population or the labor force stocks, F is the production function

growth model of Solow (1956) where production stock is $Y=AF(K,L)^1$.

Technical progress A must not be remunerated otherwise production function will not be concave. If a firm does so i.e remunerate A, then it can't survive in a competitive market because of the losses. The homogeneity character of order 1 can't hold because if the firm remunerates its inputs in their marginal productivity, then profits equals zero, it is not possible to consider A like an input like labor and capital stocks. The Euler law found neoclassical growth models and can't hold, growth models are ruled out. This aspect was examined a long time ago by Schumpeter (1942), Arrow (1962), Shell (1966, 1967, 1973), Nordhaus (1969) and Wilson (1975).

Preliminary growth models have avoided this difficulty in several ways:

Solow (1956) treats A like a public exogenous good i.e non rival and non exclusive

Shell (1966, 1967) treats A like a public good given by the government

In the both cases, A as an input can't be remunerated, the firm uses it freely. Those models integrate technological change as a non rival good, source of growth. Those models couldn't render the factor A endogenous, meaning to show that it is determinate by profit maximizing of private agents in highlighting the process which generates technological change and thus, explains long run growth.

In attempt to make the evolution of A responsive to market incentives, Arrow (1962a) assumed that an increase in physical capital necessarily leads to an equiproportionate increase in knowledge through learning by doing, but still treats knowledge as a public good. Lucas (1988) assumed in effect that it is production of human capital rather than physical capital that generates positive effects on growth.

Arrow (1962a) and Lucas (1988) make production of a non rival, non excludable good, an unintentional side effect of production of a conventional good.

Learning by doing formulation has the advantage that it makes the rate of accumulation of non rival knowledge, endogenous, but it is unsatisfactory because it takes a strict proportionality between knowledge and physical capital or knowledge and education as an unexplained and exogenously given feature of the technology. It preserves the public-good character of knowledge assumed by Solow and Shell but it makes it a public good that is privately provided as a side effect. Like the other public-good formulations, it rules out the possibility that firms make intentional investments in R&D.

Finally, Romer (1990) is a model where growth is driven by technological change that arises from intentional investment decisions made by profit-maximizing agents. The distinguishing feature of the technology as an input is that it is neither a conventional good nor a public good it is a non rival, partially excludable good. Therefore, price-taking competition cannot be supported.

The main conclusions of Romer (1990) are that the stock of human capital determinates the rate of growth, that too little human capital is devoted to research in equilibrium, that integration into world markets will increase growth rates and that having a large population is not sufficient to generate growth.

Previous literature highlights the scientific link with the study such that it is a direct application of Romer results, the study applies those results to a poor country development target. It wants to know how far it can be found a link with growth theory. As we'll see after, the finale conclusions of the analysis are close to those found by Romer. The connection with research is established since literature highlights scientific evolution of the concepts used. Once introduced, it must be improved or used to understand a given phenomenon.

4 THE MECHANICS OF ECONOMIC COMPETITIVENESS

To study the evolution of global dynamics, we determinate average per-capita knowledge of each configuration. The best way to do it is to examine the range of all of them. The methodology used is summarized in the following proposition.

Proposition 5: *global dynamics admits a upper bound* $g^{max}=g_{33}$ *as well as a lower bound,* $g^{min}=g_{11}$ *i.e*

$$g^{max}=g_{33}= \lfloor \mu \bar{\theta}^h \bar{\beta}^h /1+\bar{\theta}^h \bar{\beta}^h \rfloor_+ + \lfloor \mu \bar{\theta}^h \bar{\beta}^h /1+\bar{\theta}^h \bar{\beta}^h \rfloor_- \quad (4.1)$$

$$g^{min}=g_{11}=\mu/(1+\bar{\beta}^h)+ \left[\phi\left[\frac{\gamma\theta\beta^h}{1+\gamma\theta\beta^h}\right]^\gamma\right]^{1/2} /1+\bar{\beta}^h \quad (4.2)$$

Parameters θ and $\bar{\theta}^h$ are absent of minimum growth rate expression when the economy is globally under developed and closed. The upper bound contains those parameters because the economy is fully open.

Parameters θ and $\theta^{\bar{h}}$ act positively on the growth rate because international exchange is a growth engine. Closed economy or isolation closes markets.

High tech productivity parameter φ, the elasticity of high tech knowledge accumulation, γ as well as the low tech sector of productivity, μ act positively on global economic dynamics.

The mechanics of economic development are:

μ, the low tech sector productivity

φ, the high tech sector productivity

γ, knowledge accumulation externality

In parallel, the mechanics of under development are :

β^b is the discount rate of high tech goods

$\beta^{\bar{h}}$ is the discount rate of low tech goods

The beginning of market increases size needs fixed cost and new investments.

5 CONCLUSION

This chapter characterizes global dynamics of the economy like a random process difficult to predict over time. Therefore, crucial parameters are difficult to highlight and predict because of the multiple equilibria.

Indeed, complete endogenous technological change raises uncertainty in political economic terms because of multiple trajectories which may take the economy. The best way to study global dynamics is to collect some information which may explain the economic behavior in respect to the parameters found for a given range and see in how far the strategy used may be considered successful.

Next chapter looks for existence of an unique global dynamics equilibrium in order to conclude on economic policy efficiency proposed here for development and long run growth.

Chapitre N° 4

International exchange dynamics and economic development

1 PARTIAL ENDOGENOUS KNOWLEDGE

In partial endogenous knowledge, total stock of intermediate goods that high tech firm is willing to get is located at E. Respective earnings generated by high quality goods from developed or developing countries are denoted w_t^B and w_t^A respectively, the profit generated is π_t. The acquisition decision of intermediate goods results from benefit comparisons.

1.1 Increasing earnings

1    $w_t^A \succ w_t^B$

-If purchase occurs then if $0<\theta\leq 1$ and $0<p<1$, information is not perfect for rational choice to be made. Therefore per-capita knowledge converges at least to h^*, thus economy is locates to the take-off frontier. National goods preferred don't have enough quality compare to average world's quality because it is already discarded. Economy stabilizes at a low relative per-capita knowledge level. If p converges to *1* then it widen the market size which leads to the increase of θ then dynamics path of the economy keeps increasing.

-Purchase didn't occur, then if $\theta > 1$ and $p=1$, information is perfect and enough to deny the purchase of intermediate good because its quality is below the one which prevails in the international market. Thus, full open economy leads to skills convergence through understanding of the technology contained in goods.

The impact on the growth rate

Using high tech firm production function (chapter 2), we illustrate results of the analysis: there exists a positive parameter τ such that:

$w_t^B = (1-\tau) w_t^A$

Exchange terms establishes like (1.1) i.e

$$\zeta^2 = \beta^h [(\theta-1)p+1] \ln(w_t^A h_{t+1}) \qquad (1.1)$$

we have seen that in that case, we necessary have $0<p<1$ or $p=1$ for θ to be included in the analysis.

If $\zeta<0$, then exchange terms are altered because $\beta^h[(\theta-1)p+1]ln(w_t^A h_{t+1})<0$ i.e $\beta^h[(\theta-1)p+1]<0$ necessarily because the log function is always positive, therefore we have $\beta^h<0$ or $[(\theta-1)p+1]<0$

-In the second case exchange terms are altered because if $p=1$ then $0<\theta<1$ is opposite to the strategy conducted because full open of the economy is coupled to good exchange restrictions. If $0<p<1$ then $\theta>1$ i.e low opening is coupled to high exchanges, demand is higher than supply which means that demand for high quality goods are not

---

[2] $\zeta=F_t^H-ln(1-e_t)-\beta^h p\theta ln(1-\tau)$

effective[3] because they only express hopes due to capital absence.

-If $\beta^h < 0$ i.e the discount rate is negative, then investments are not interesting because of non profitability.

$\zeta > 0$, exchange terms have improved, thus $\beta^h[(\theta-1)p+1]\ln(w_t^A h_{t+1}) > 0$ i.e $\beta^h[(\theta-1)p+1] > 0$. Therefore, $\beta^h > 0$ and $[(\theta-1)p+1] > 0$

-In the second case, exchange terms have improved because if $p=1$, we necessary have $\theta > 1$, because great opening increase freedom in good exchanges. Funds allocated to intermediate goods are available, exchange terms are good. Otherwise if $0 < p < 1$, given that $[(\theta-1)p+1] > 0$ then

---

[3] See the general theory Keynes (1936)

$\theta \succ 0$, partial opening of the economy is associated to exchanges equity, therefore the demands are effective because funds are available.

-If $\beta^h > 0$ then the investments are interesting

2   $w_t^A < w_t^B$

-Purchase has been done, then $\theta \succ 1$ and $p=1$ because of the occurrence of convergence in per-capita knowledge. If this increase keeps going, then there is monopoly rent seeking broke down which rules out of equilibrium in terms of intermediate goods exchange due to high foreign goods preferences. Therefore, relationships among the firms are unbalanced and slow the economic dynamics evolution to its long run.

-Purchase wasn't done, thus, $\theta=0$ and $p=0$ which means that the economy as well as the firms are isolated from the rest of the world. There are not external effects generated by the touch with over countries specifically in goods.

3   Now, we have $w_t^B=(1+\tau)w_t^A$

1.2.1 The impact on the growth rate

Like viewed in the above cases, exchanges terms are expressed by $\zeta=\beta^b[(\theta-1)p+1]ln(w_t^A h_{t+1})$, the analysis is conducts like following

If $w_t^B \approx w_t^A$

-If purchase occurs, when $p=1$ if $\theta>1$, then per-capita knowledge converges to $\hat{h}$

-If purchase occurs, when $0<p<1$ if $0<\theta\leq1$, then per-capita knowledge converges to h^*

-If purchase didn't occurs when $p=1$ if $\theta=0$, then per-capita knowledge converges to $h_0<h^*$ if $\theta<1$, then purchase occurs at a low probability due to a low opening leading to asymmetric information which can't allow a rational purchase choice. Therefore, per-capita knowledge stagnates and converges to $h_0<h^*$

1.3.1 The impact on the growth rate

Exchange terms expression is

$$\zeta = \beta^h [1 + p(\theta-1)] \ln(w_t h_{t+1}) \qquad (1.2)$$

Exchange rate alteration means that $\zeta = \beta^h [1 + p(\theta-1)] \ln(w_t^A h_{t+1}) < 0$ which implies $\beta^h < 0$ or $[1 + p(\theta-1)] < 0$

$\beta^h < 0$ means that dual investments are not interesting

$[1 + p(\theta-1)] < 0$ means that $p(\theta-1) < 1$ which implies $\theta < 1$ if $0 < p < 1$, opening is holding or the economy is out of the international market because there are not any goods exchanged, $\theta < 0$ if $p = 1$, there have been a conflict because opening is effective but no exchanges are done.

Exchange terms improve i.e

$\zeta = \beta^b[1+p(\theta-1)]ln(w_i^A h_{i+1}) \succ 0$ therefore $\beta^b \succ 0$ and $[1+p(\theta-1)] \succ 0$

$\beta^b \succ 0$ means that dual investments are interesting

$[1+p(\theta-1)] \succ 0$ means that $p(\theta-1) \succ 0$ i.e $\theta \succ 1$ if $0<p<1$ then the economy is opening and it is well connected to the international market because exchanges levels are high, $\theta \succeq 1$ if $p=1$, then the exchanges are balanced

2 COMPLETE ENDOGENOUS TECHNOLOGY

In complete endogenous technology, total stock of the intermediate goods of both low and high techs firms is higher than in partial endogenous technology, respective earns of the both low and the high tech sectors are w_t^B and w_t^A as well as $w_t^{0,B}$ and $w_t^{0,A}$ which leads to the profits rates π_t and π_t^0, the final decision results from the comparison of earns.

2.1 The joint analysis

Proposition: *global economic dynamics in complete endogenous technology admits a unique equilibrium such that :*

$\varphi =$

$\beta^h\left[(\theta-1)p+1\right]\ln\left(w_t^A h_{t+1}\right) + \beta^{\bar{h}}\left[(\bar{\theta}-1)q+1\right]\ln\left(w_t^{0,A} h_{t+1}^0\right)$

(2.1)

To prove this result, note the validity of following array

	$w_t^B \succ w_t^A$	$w_t^B < w_t^A$	$w_t^B = w_t^A$
$w_t^{0,B} \succ w_t^{0,A}$	$(w_t^{0,B}, w_t^{0,A}) \cap (w_t^B \succ w_t^A)$	$(w_t^{0,B} \succ w_t^{0,A}) \cap (w_t^B < w_t^A)$	$(w_t^{0,B} \succ w_t^{0,A}) \cap (w_t^B = w_t^A)$
$w_t^{0,B} < w_t^{0,A}$	$(w_t^{0,B} < w_t^{0,A}) \cap (w_t^B \succ w_t^A)$	$(w_t^{0,B} < w_t^{0,A}) \cap (w_t^B < w_t^A)$	$(w_t^{0,B} < w_t^{0,A}) \cap (w_t^B = w_t^A)$
$w_t^{0,B} = w_t^{0,A}$	$(w_t^{0,B} = w_t^{0,A}) \cap (w_t^B \succ w_t^A)$	$(w_t^{0,B} = w_t^{0,A}) \cap (w_t^B < w_t^A)$	$(w_t^{0,B} = w_t^{0,A}) \cap (w_t^B = w_t^A)$

It can be given a probability law, ζ_{ij} at each configuration where

	$w_t^B \succ w_t^A$	$w_t^B < w_t^A$	$w_t^B = w_t^A$
$w_t^{0,B} \succ w_t^{0,A}$	ζ_{11}	ζ_{12}	ζ_{13}
$w_t^{0,B} < w_t^{0,A}$	ζ_{21}	ζ_{22}	ζ_{23}
$w_t^{0,B} = w_t^{0,A}$	ζ_{31}	ζ_{32}	ζ_{33}

If we apply the methodology viewed above, we can see that all the joined law are the same, therefore $\zeta_{ij} = \varphi$ where

$$\varphi = \beta^h[(\theta-1)p+1]\ln(w_t^A h_{t+1}^A) + \beta^{\bar{h}}[(\theta^{\bar{h}}-1)q+1]\ln(w_t^{0,A} h_{t+1}^0)$$

Therefore, the methodology used in this study is a parallel of the methodology of previous chapters but this current methodology is simpler because the earnings have no impact on the study of evolution of global dynamics when economy is fully open. We need to identify parameters of economic development.

$\forall\ w_t^B,\ w_t^A,\ w_t^{0,B},\ w_t^{0,A}$ are respective earnings on intermediate goods of the countries A (poor) and B (rich) for the high and the low tech firms.

Exchange terms are altered if $\phi<0$ i.e
$\beta^h[(\theta-1)p+1]<0$ and
$\beta^{\bar{h}}[(\theta^{\bar{h}}-1)q+1]<0$

-The first case was studied above and for the second case, the exchange terms are altered because

$\beta^{\bar{h}} [(\theta^{\bar{h}} -1)q+1]<0$ which implies
$\beta^b<0$ or $[(\theta-1)p+1]<0$

-In the second case, the exchange terms are altered because if $q=1$, then $0<\theta^{\bar{h}}<1$ contradict the logic of the strategy highlighted where a great open is coupled to great international exchanges, the current means that financial funds are available but there exist other kind of block parameters not highlighted economically.

Otherwise if $0<q<1$ then $\theta^{\bar{h}}>1$ which means that a great opening of the economy is coupled to high demand, therefore the demand is higher than the supply because they are not effective[4] due to the financial funds absence.

-If $\bar{\beta^h} < 0$, the discount rate is negative which means that the investments are too costly

Exchange terms are positive if $\phi > 0$ i.e
$\beta^b[(\theta-1)p+1] \succ 0$ and $\bar{\beta^h}[(\bar{\theta^h}-1)q+1] \succ 0$

Dealing with the second case, it came out that

$\bar{\beta^h}[(\bar{\theta^h}-1)q+1] \succ 0$ which yields to

$\bar{\beta^h} \succ 0$ and $(\bar{\theta^h}-1)q+1 \succ 0$

-In the second case, exchange terms are <u>altered because if $q=1$</u>, then there only

[4] See Keynes (1936)

exists $\bar{\theta}^h$ which leads to, $\bar{\theta}^h > 1$ necessarily. Therefore, a great open leads to good exchanges freedom, the financial funds are enough and the exchange terms are positive.

Otherwise if $0<q<1$, given $[(\bar{\theta}^h - 1)q+1] > 0$ then

$\bar{\theta}^h > 0$, a great opening of the economy is associated to the equilibrium exchanges. Demand equals supply of dual good and therefore demands are effective because funds are available.

- $\bar{\beta}^h > 0$ means that the investments are interesting.

2.2 The mechanics of economic development

To determinate the conditional laws of the analysis, observe the following array. The aim is to make sure that the international exchanges as a positive impact on growth and development.

2.2.2 The study of the dynamics of ψ_{11} where $\psi_{11} = \beta^h \beta^{\bar{h}}$

Exchange terms are positive if $\psi_{11} > 0$ i.e
$\beta^h > 0$ and $\beta^{\bar{h}} > 0$

Exchange terms are altered if $\psi_{11} < 0$ i.e
$\beta^h < 0$ and $\beta^{\bar{h}} > 0$ or
$\beta^{\bar{h}} > 0$ and $\beta^h < 0$

2.2.3 Study of the dynamics of ψ_{12} where

$$\psi_{12} = \beta^b[(\theta^{\bar{h}}-1)q+1]$$

Exchange terms are positive if $\psi_{12} > 0$ i.e
$\beta^b > 0$ and $[(\theta^{\bar{h}}-1)q+1] > 0$

Exchange terms are altered if $\psi_{12} < 0$ i.e
$\beta^b < 0$ and $[(\theta^{\bar{h}}-1)q+1] > 0$ or
$\beta^b > 0$ and $[(\theta^{\bar{h}}-1)q+1] < 0$

2.2.4 Study of the dynamics of ψ_{21}
where $\psi_{21} = [(\theta-1)p+1]\beta^{\bar{h}}$

Exchange terms are positive if $\psi_{21} > 0$ i.e
$[(\theta-1)p+1] > 0$ and $\beta^{\bar{h}} > 0$

Exchange terms are altered if $\psi_{21} < 0$ i.e

$[(\theta-1)p+1]<0$ and $\beta^{\bar{h}}>0$ or

$[(\theta-1)p+1]>0$ and $\beta^{\bar{h}}<0$

2.2.5 Study of the dynamics of ψ_{22}

where

$\psi_{22}=[(\theta-1)p+1][(\theta^{\bar{h}}-1)q+1]$

Exchange terms are positive if $\psi_{22}>0$ i.e

$[(\theta-1)p+1]>0$ and $[(\theta^{\bar{h}}-1)q+1]>0$

Exchange terms are altered if $\psi_{22}<0$ i.e

$[(\theta-1)p+1]>0$ and $[(\theta^{\bar{h}}-1)q+1]<0$ or

$[(\theta-1)p+1]<0$ and $[(\theta^{\bar{h}}-1)q+1]>0$

2.2.6 Homogenous definition

Finally exchange rates are positive if

$\{\beta^h \succ 0, \beta^{\bar{h}} \succ 0\}$

$\cup \{\beta^h \succ 0, [(\theta^{\bar{h}}-1)q+1] \succ 0\}$

$\cup \{[(\theta-1)p+1] \succ 0, \beta^{\bar{h}} \succ 0\}$

$\cup \{[(\theta-1)p+1] \succ 0, [(\theta^{\bar{h}}-1)q+1] \succ 0\}$

$\cup \{[(\theta-1)p+1] \succ 0, [(\theta^{\bar{h}}-1)q+1] \succ 0\}$

Proposition: *the mechanics of economic development are: low tech and the high tech discount rates, β^h and $\beta^{\bar{h}}$,*

Opening degree of economy in regard to high and low tech firms parameters: p and q

The parameters of preference in respect to the high and the low tech sectors: θ et $\theta^{\bar{h}}$

When we closed economy in the first chapter, the system highlighted multiple equilibria where the parameters β^h and $\beta^{\bar{h}}$ where not positive for the economy because it was the beginning of the policy which leads fixed cost.

Conclusion

The finale close of the model of complete endogenous technology highlights a unique equilibrium. All economic configurations share the same long run solution. Therefore international exchange is crucial, highlights terms of negotiation with the rest of the world.

The economic dynamics is a saddle path which converges to the same locus, therefore unique equilibrium is stable because all the paths go to the same locus.

Increasing returns widen market size. Chapter 3 built factors endowment of country in order to face international trade and win. The application of comparative advantages in international exchange determinates a unique stable solution highlights using knowledge external effects.

Consequently, integration of poor economy in world market is a necessity for growth and development. Population size doesn't increase growth and development. Our results converge to those of Romer (1990)

This model can be used to examine political impact on the opening degree of countries in order to unify politics and economics and to see if there is a convergence and/ or if they can be used for development in macro level (the country) or in micro level (the firms). Consumers can be introduced too in order to model explicitly human capital accumulation or study impact of population behavior on development and growth.

Table of Content

Presentation

Chapter 1. The preliminary Analysis
    1. Presentation
    2. The literature of the model

Chapter 2. Partial endogenous technological change
    1. Definition
    2. The analytic methodology
    3. Determination of knowledge dynamics
    4. Macroeconomics interpretation of the analysis
    5. Global dynamics evolution

6. The stages of economic development

7. Poverty and under development

8. Economic competitiveness

9. Conclusion

Chapter 3. The strategy of economic development

1. Complete endogenous technology

2. Evolution of the economic dynamics

3. The global dynamics

4. The mechanics of economic competitiveness

5. Conclusion

Chapter 4. International exchange dynamics and economic development

1. Partial endogenous knowledge

2. Complete endogenous technology

Conclusion

References

Bibliographie

Aghion, P. and Howitt, P., Théorie de la Croissance, 1998, Dunod

Assidon, Elsa, 2002, Les Théories Economiques du développement, Repères, la Découverte

Brunel, S., Le Sud dans la Nouvelle Economie Mondiale, PUF

Burki, A. and Terrel, D., 1998, Measuring production efficiency of small firms in Pakistan, World Development, 26 (1), 155-169

Cass, D., Optimum Growth in an Aggregate Model of Capital Accumulation, Review of Economic Studies, 32, 233-240

Chou, S.Y., Grossman., M., Saffer, H., 2003, An economic analysis of adult obesity results from the behavioral risk factor surveillance system, Journal of health economics, 23 (3), 565-587

Collins, J. and Porras, J., 1994, Built to last: Successful habits of visionary companies, New-York: Harper and Collins

Cutler, D.M., Glaeser, E.L., Shapiro, J.M., 2003, Why have Americans become more obese? Journal of Economic Perspectives, 17 (3), 93-118

Doquier, F. and Rapoport, H., 2010, Glabalization, Brain-Drain and Development, Journal of Economic Literature

Docquier, F; and Marfouk, A., 2006, International Migration by educational attainment, Palgrave Mc Millan New-york

Downing, J. and Daniels, L., 1992, The growth and dynamics of women entrepreneurs in Southern Africa, GEMINI, technical report number 27, Washington D.C. US AID

Fleming, J.M., 1955, External Economics and the doctrine of Balanced Growth, Economic Journal, June

Goel, R.K., 2006, Obesity: an economic and financial perspective, Journal of Economics and Finance, 30 (3), 317-324

Goldmark, L. and Barber, T., 2005, Trade micro and small enterprises and global value chain. AMAP report number 25, Washington D.C. US AID

Hirschman, A., 1958, The Stategy of Economic Development, New Haven, Conn: Yale University Press

Hugon, P., 1999, L'Economie de l'Afrique, Repères, la Découverte

King, R. G., Rebelo, S., 1990, Public Policy and Economic Growth: Developing Neoclassical Implications, NBER Working Paper n°3338

Krugman, 1994, The Fall and rise of Development economics, working paper, p.1-13

Koopmans, T, 1965, On the Concept of Optimal growth, The Econometrics Approach to Development Planning, Chicago

Levy, A., 2002, Rational eating: can it lead to overweightness or underweightness? , Journal of health economics, 21 (5), 887-899

Lewis, W.A., 1954, Economic Development with unlimited supplies of Labor, The Manchester School, May

Leadholm, C., 2002, Small firm dynamics: Evidence from Africa and Latin America, Small Business Economics, 18 (3), 227-242

Lucas R.E., On the Mechanics of Economic Development, Journal of Monetary Economics, 22, 3-42

Myrdal, G; 1957, Economic Theory and Under-developed Regions, London, Duckworth

Parker, J., 1995, Partners of Business Growth, Micro and Small Enterprises in Kenya, ph.D Dissertation

Philipson, T.J., Posner, R.A., 1999, The long-run growth in obesity as a function of technological change. Working Paper 7423. National Bureau of Economic Research, Cambridge, MA

Rashad, I., Grossman, Chou, S.Y., 2006, The Super Size of America: an economic estimation of body mass index and obesity in adults, Eastern Economic Journal, 32 (1), 133-148

Romer, P., 1986, Increasing Returns and Long Run Growth, Journal of Political Economy 94, 1002-1037

Romer, P. 1990, Progrès Technique Endogène, Annales d'Economie et Statistiques, N°22, 1991

Roseinstein-Rodan, P., 1943, Problem of Industrialization of Eastern and Sout-Easter Europe, Economic Journal, June

Tan, H. and Batra, G., 1995, technical efficiency of SME , World Bank, Washington D.C

Wigniolle, B., 2005, Does Imperfect Competition Foster Capital Accumulation in a Developing Economy?, Cahier de la MSE

Young, A., 1928, Increasing Returns and Economic Progress, December

Zon, A., Muysken, J., 2001, Health and endogenous Growth, Journal of Health Economics, 20, 169-1

www.ingramcontent.com/pod-product-compliance
Lightning Source LLC
Chambersburg PA
CBHW021942170526
45157CB00003B/897